A New Sound

When letters are put together, sometimes they form new sounds. For example, think about the sound the letter **t** makes. Then think about the sound the letter **h** makes. But put them together and we have a new sound called a **consonant digraph**.

 tee**th**   fea**th**er

Say each word. Circle the consonant digraph in each word.

cheese	shape	thing	whistle
wish	what	chop	both
they	chief	math	wheel
show	mother	teach	cheer

Underline the consonant digraphs in the words. Write a sentence using each word.

fish _____

_____

chair _____

_____

this _____

_____

when _____

_____

What's Missing?

Finish each word using the consonant digraphs **ch**, **sh**, **th**, or **wh**.
Write the complete word on the line.

1. __ __ i r t   _____

2. t o u __ __   _____

3. s p i n a __ __   _____

4. f i n i __ __   _____

5. h e a l __ __   _____

6. __ __ i c k e n   _____

7. __ __ e n e v e r   _____

8. b a __ __   _____

9. __ __ i n k   _____

10. d i __ __   _____

Recognizing consonant digraphs

Building from the Root

We can create a new word by adding a **prefix** to the beginning of the root word.

prefix	+	root word	=	new word
un		happy		**un**happy

prefix	meaning
un	**not**
re	**back or again**
pre	**before**

Add the prefix **un**, **re**, or **pre** to each root word to make a new word.

Root Word	New Word	Root Word	New Word
try	_____	intended	_____
common	_____	view	_____
cook	_____	wash	_____
organized	_____	appear	_____
harmed	_____	plan	_____
consider	_____	breakable	_____
test	_____	likely	_____

Super Suffixes!

We can create a new word by adding a **suffix** to the end of the root word.

root word   +   **suffix**   =   **new word**
bake   er   bak**er**

suffix	meaning
er	a person who
est	most
full	full of
less	without

Add the suffix **er**, **est**, **ful**, or **less** to each root word to make a new word.

Root Word	New Word	Root Word	New Word
help	_____	peace	_____
produce	_____	care	_____
smart	_____	great	_____
hope	_____	buy	_____
play	_____	drive	_____
thought	_____	waste	_____
manage	_____	fish	_____

Adding suffixes

Take Action on Contractions

The word contract means to make smaller. A **contraction** is a word made up of two words that are put together and made into a shorter word. An apostrophe takes the place of the letters that are taken out of the word.

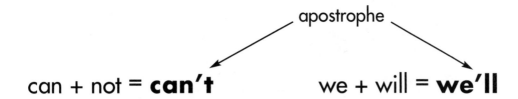

can + not = **can't**   we + will = **we'll**

Add the two words to make a contraction.

First word	Second word	Contraction
1. we	are	we're
2. they	are	_____
3. she	is	_____
4. he	is	_____
5. I	am	_____
6. we	have	_____
7. they	have	_____
8. I	have	_____
9. she	has	_____
10. he	has	_____
11. can	not	_____
12. should	not	_____
13. would	not	_____
14. could	not	_____

Similar Synonyms

Words that have the same or nearly the same meaning are called **synonyms**.

fast  **speedy**

Draw a line to match the synonyms.

big	yell
woman	large
happy	lady
shout	wish
great	glad
hope	leap
jump	excellent

Write two **synonyms** to describe each picture.

_____   _____

_____   _____

Opposites Attract

Words that have the opposite meaning are called **antonyms**.

big  **little**

Draw a line to match the antonyms.

up	happy
sad	weak
whisper	down
strong	exit
tall	shout
enter	off
on	short

Write a word to describe each picture. Then write an **antonym** for the word.

_____

Antonym: _____   Antonym: _____

Write it Right!

Words that sound the same but have a different spelling and meaning are called **homophones**.

meet  **meat**

Read each sentence carefully and circle the correct homophone to complete it. Then rewrite the sentence on the line.

1. I (knew, new) that going to the park would be fun._____

_____

2. The (son, sun) and daughter walked with their parents._____

_____

3. He dug a (whole, hole) to plant the tree._____

_____

4. Jeff said there is (know, no) more ice cream._____

_____

5. We went to the store to (bye, buy, by) new clothes._____

_____

6. "Let's go over (there, they're, their)!" Lucy shouted._____

_____

7. They came over to (hour, our) house to play._____

_____

8. Alecia asked if everyone could (hear, here) her._____

_____

9. The Mustangs (won, one) the championship._____

_____

10. (Your, You're) my best friend._____

_____

Recognizing Homophones

Compound Connection

Words that are made up of two smaller words are called **compound words**.

dog + house = **doghouse**

Write a compound word by putting each pair of words together.

1. home + work = _____

2. some + one = _____

3. sun + shine = _____

4. grand + parents = _____

5. night + light = _____

6. sun + set = _____

7. in + side = _____

8. cook + book = _____

9. birth + day = _____

10. play + ground = _____

11. sea + shell = _____

12. sail + boat = _____

13. pan + cake = _____

14. grape + fruit = _____

15. cow + boy = _____

Instructions Included

Read each sentence carefully and follow the directions.

Write your name below the line. _____

Use the circle to draw a face.
First, draw two eyes, a nose,
and a mouth.
Next, draw two ears.
Finally, draw some hair.

Write the numbers 1 through 10 to the right.
Write the odd numbers in the box and the
even numbers on top of the box.

Draw a square above the line
and to the left of the star.

Draw a circle inside the triangle
but outside the square.

Turn this letter J into a smile face.
Draw two dots for eyes on either
side of it and a smile below it.

J

Main Idea Mystery

A group of sentences that tells about an idea or thought is called a **paragraph**. The **main idea** is the most important part of a paragraph. A paragraph is made up of a main idea and supporting sentences.

Read each paragraph and write the main idea.

Pizza is a healthy food. One reason is because it has a good balance of the food pyramid. It has crust, tomato sauce, and cheese. It can also have meat and vegetables.

Main Idea

The giant panda is a fascinating animal. It lives in China in the mountains and uses its special paws to eat bamboo. Because bamboo is not very nutritious, the panda must eat as much as 20 pounds of bamboo each day. The giant panda population has decreased greatly since the early 1900s. This is because the panda has been hunted for fur and accidentally killed in traps set for other animals. The people of China have set up areas for pandas to live in safely. Also, it is against the law to hunt the giant panda.

Main Idea

Making chocolate chip cookies can be a lot of fun. First, you preheat the oven to 350 degrees and grease the cookie sheets. Mix butter-flavored shortening, brown sugar, and white sugar in a large bowl until they are light and fluffy. Then add eggs one at a time and beat them well while stirring in vanilla. Mix in flour, baking soda, and salt and slowly stir until creamy. Finally, fold in the chocolate chips. Now you are ready to drop the cookie dough onto the cookie sheets. Use rounded spoonfuls. Bake the cookies for 8 to 10 minutes, until light brown. When they are done baking, allow the cookies to cool on the baking sheet for 5 minutes before moving them to a wire rack to cool completely.

Main Idea

Details, Details

Details tell more about the main idea.

Read each paragraph. Underline the main idea. Circle the supporting details.

Reading is important for many reasons. It helps you to learn new things that you can share with others. Plus, it is fun! You can pick up a book and take an adventure, go on a journey, or meet new friends. Reading also helps you to become a better speller and writer. Reading is a skill that helps you do well in school, and doing well in school will help you be successful in everything you do. With practice, you can become a better reader.

Recycling helps make our world a healthier and safer place. Many people recycle plastic, aluminum, and paper. This reduces the amount of trash that is sent to landfills. Because we have a limited amount of space on Earth, it helps to recycle. So we should recycle as much as we can!

We have rules and laws for two very important reasons. First, they provide organization. Without organization there would be confusion, which could cause many problems. We also have rules and laws to protect us and keep us safe. It is important to follow them to keep people from getting hurt and their property from being damaged or stolen.

Super Supporting Details

Read each main idea. Write two or three sentences with details that support the main idea.

Eating healthy food is important for many reasons. _____

_____

_____

_____

_____

It is important for children to get about nine or ten hours of sleep every night.

_____

_____

_____

_____

_____

Throwing away your trash at the park is important for many reasons.

_____

_____

_____

_____

_____

Describe It!

Think of a topic that you are interested in. It could be a hobby, an animal, or a person. Write your topic in the main idea circle. Then write four facts about your topic in the detail boxes.

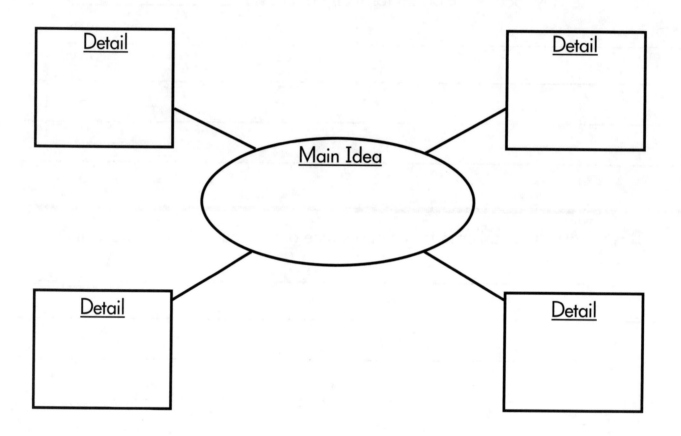

Write a paragraph using your main topic and supporting details.

_____

_____

_____

_____

_____

_____

_____

Writing a descriptive paragraph

You Be the Writer

Select a topic from the box below and write it in the main idea circle. Then write four facts about your topic in the detail boxes.

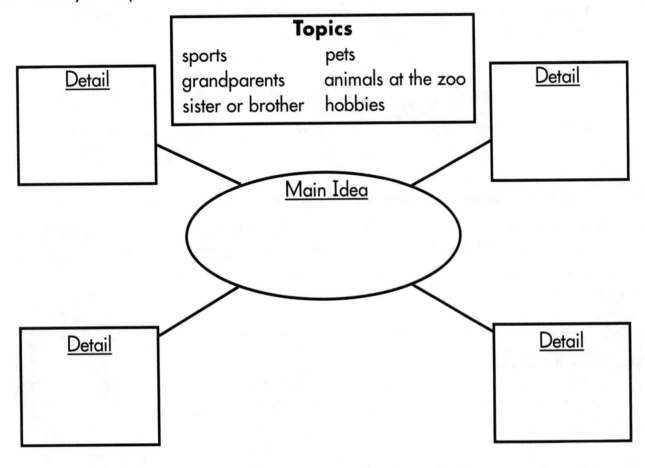

Topics

sports   pets
grandparents   animals at the zoo
sister or brother   hobbies

Detail

Detail

Main Idea

Detail

Detail

Write a paragraph using your main topic and supporting details.

_____

_____

_____

_____

_____

_____

What's in a Sentence?

A sentence must begin with a capital letter and end with a period (.), exclamation point (!), or question mark (?). Also, every sentence must have a **naming part** and an **action part**. The naming part tells who or what the sentence is about. The action part tells what the naming part does or is.

capital letter

period

The dogs bark.

naming part

action part

Read each group of words below. If it is a complete sentence, circle it and draw a line to match the sentence with its picture. If it is not a complete sentence, rewrite it as one.

We a game.

_____

We played at the park.

_____

We won the game!

_____

Game over.

_____

Mom watched the game

_____

She cheered!

_____

The team had ice cream.

_____

Love ice cream!

_____

Identifying complete sentences

Making Sentences Complete

Rewrite each group of words to make it a complete sentence.

1. lena went to the store to buy flowers

   Lena went to the store to buy flowers.

2. ben his mom if they could go to the store.

   _____

3. Lauren and her brother played in the yard

   _____

4. is teaching her how to knit.

   _____

5. grandpa woke up early to go fishing.

   _____

Write complete sentences using the words in the box. Only use each word or group of words once.

went to the library	took a boat to the island	Gary and Michelle	Shelly and I
played in the clubhouse	stood in line for an hour	Jonathan	We
skated to my house		The whole class	

6. _____

7. _____

8. _____

9. _____

10. _____

It Takes Two

Every sentence has two main parts. The naming part, or the part that tells who the sentence is about, is called the **subject**. The action part, or the part that tells what the subject does or is, is called the **predicate**.

<u>**Lions roar.**</u>
subject   predicate

Read each sentence. Circle the subject and underline the predicate.

1. Our class went on a field trip to the zoo.

2. We bought our tickets and went in through the front gate.

3. The teacher divided our class up into small groups.

4. I was in the group with my two best friends.

5. We went to see the koalas first.

6. Emma wanted to see the elephants next.

7. Our group stopped at a park bench to have a snack while we watched the giraffes.

8. Jeanie and Lily wanted to see the cheetahs.

9. Mrs. Johnson said it was time to meet our class back at the front entrance.

10. We had a great time and learned a whole lot about the different animals we saw.

Spectacular Subjects

Write a subject from the list to complete each sentence. Use each subject only once.

The truck	The Smiths
We	Alexis and Karen
Grandma and grandpa	Ashley
The pet shop	Jack and Alan
Our class	The team

1. _____ walked home from school today.

2. _____ are on the same baseball team.

3. _____ earned an extra recess for excellent behavior.

4. _____ brought all the furniture to their new house.

5. _____ has practically every species of fish!

6. _____ played outside all day.

7. _____ built a new clubhouse in their backyard.

8. _____ ordered a new red car.

9. _____ thought they played their best game yet.

10. _____ watched a movie on Saturday afternoon.

Powerful Predicates

Write a predicate from the list to complete each sentence. Use each predicate only once.

> *went to the playground with her babysitter.*
> *broke when my brother threw it on the floor.*
> *planted a colorful bush in their garden.*
> *was having a huge sale.*
> *had fun at the parade.*
> *enjoyed the beautiful sunshine today.*
> *was playing my favorite song.*
> *is a healthy snack.*
> *was very relaxing.*
> *went to the pool for the day.*

1. They _____

2. The toy _____

3. We _____

4. The radio _____

5. My family _____

6. Jessica _____

7. An apple _____

8. The vacation _____

9. The store _____

10. Their friends _____

Adding a predicate to complete a sentence

Know Your Nouns

A **noun** is a person, place, or thing.

person   place   thing

Circle all the nouns in each sentence.

1. Mr. Green planted a vegetable garden last weekend.

2. The garden is filled with lettuce and tomatoes.

3. Broccoli and carrots are growing, too.

4. Mr. Green waters the garden every day.

5. My mother asked Mr. Green for some tomatoes.

6. The bunnies in the neighborhood like the carrots.

7. Mr. Green put up a fence to keep the bunnies out.

8. One bunny squeezed under the fence.

9. The bunny ate two carrots.

10. Mr. Green chased the bunny out of the garden.

Proper Noun Town

A **proper noun** names a specific person, place, or thing. Proper nouns always begin with a capital letter.

Mr. Green

Circle all the proper nouns in each sentence.

1. Where does your Grandma Shirley live?

2. She lives in Pittsburgh, Pennsylvania.

3. Her house is on Oak Street.

4. Every year the Wilson family goes to Florida.

5. They have lots of fun swimming in the Atlantic Ocean.

6. David turns ten this year.

7. His birthday is in July.

8. David wants to go to Midtown Bowling for his birthday.

Think of a proper noun for each noun. Write it on the line.

a person _____   a month _____

a city _____   a team _____

a library _____   a game _____

a book _____   a store _____

a teacher _____   a restaurant _____

Two or More

A noun that names more than one person, place, or thing is called a **plural noun**.

There are four different ways to make a noun plural.

For most nouns, add **s**		For nouns that end in **x, z, ch,** or **sh,** add **es**	
hat	hat<u>s</u>	box	box<u>es</u>

For nouns that end with a consonant **y** pattern, change the **y** to **i** and add **es**		Irregular plural	
party	part<u>ies</u>	child	children

Look at the ending of each noun. Make the noun plural and write it on the line.

computer _____   box _____

book _____   ditch _____

watch _____   puppy _____

goose _____   table _____

candy _____   swing _____

boat _____   dish _____

lily _____   freeze _____

fox _____   itch _____

wish _____   door _____

sandwich _____   light _____

tree _____   clubhouse _____

Get Personal with Pronouns

Pronouns are words that take the place of nouns.

(She)
<u>Emily</u> gave the books to Alex.

She gave the books to Alex.

Pronouns
I   he   she   we   they   it   you

Read the sentences. Underline the nouns and circle the pronouns.

1. The sunset was a shade of pinkish orange. It was beautiful.

2. The sky was clear. It was blue.

3. The sailboats drifted on the water. They moved quickly.

4. Johnny wanted to go on the boat. Mom said it wasn't safe.

5. Johnny stayed at home. He played with Billy.

6. Sam caught a fish. It was pretty big.

7. Sam struggled with the fish. Mom watched him.

8. Dad and Sam put the fish in a bucket. They brought it home.

9. The fish had a funny smell. It wasn't good.

10. Mom cooked the fish. Then Dad and Sam ate it.

Subject Switch

Some pronouns take the place of nouns in the subject of the sentence.

Lucy rode her bike to school.
She rode her bike to school.

Write a pronoun that can take the place of the underlined nouns.

1. _____ <u>Andrew</u> was supposed to wash the chalkboard.

2. _____ <u>Richard and I</u> are going to do it instead.

3. _____ <u>Jamie and Hannah</u> are in charge of cleaning the erasers.

4. _____ <u>The pencil sharpener</u> needed to be emptied.

5. _____ <u>Grace</u> emptied the trash.

6. _____ <u>Everyone in the class</u> pitched in to help.

7. _____ <u>Ted</u> took a message to the office.

8. _____ <u>Danny and Natalie</u> put books away in the library.

9. _____ <u>Our desks</u> were dirty so we cleaned them.

10. _____ <u>The classroom</u> looked great when we were finished.

Trading Nouns for Pronouns

Some pronouns take the place of nouns that come after a verb.

The bus driver gave <u>the students</u> a treat on the last day of school.

SCHOOL BUS

The bus driver gave **them** a treat on the last day of school.

Pronouns

me	you	him	her	it	us	them

Write a pronoun that can take the place of the underlined nouns.

1. _____ Janet called <u>Shelby</u> to invite her over to her house.

2. _____ The principal asked <u>Mrs. Jones</u> to bring her class first.

3. _____ Mrs. Cole spoke to <u>Brian</u> about using table manners.

4. _____ Leo shared <u>a birthday treat</u> with the whole class.

5. _____ My mom called <u>Billy and me</u> in for dinner.

6. _____ We got <u>the new CD</u> from the music store.

7. _____ We had fun playing <u>the computer game</u>.

8. _____ Grandma went to <u>the baseball game</u> with us.

9. _____ Lisa helped <u>her family</u> rearrange the furniture.

10. _____ Abby was crying because she hurt <u>her foot</u> on the sidewalk.

Using pronouns in place of nouns

Take Action with Verbs

A **verb** tells what a person or thing does.

The gorilla **pounds** on its chest.

Circle all the verbs in each sentence.

1. The grizzly bear sneaked into the cave.

2. We watched the koala climb the tree with ease.

3. The parrot flew from one tree to another.

4. The zookeeper fed the elephants.

5. The monkeys acted silly when they saw us watching them!

6. The seals glided through the water quickly.

7. The cheetah ran as fast as lightning.

8. We learned that the kangaroo uses its tail for balance.

9. The penguins slid on the ice.

10. The lion roared at us!

Write a sentence using each verb.

reach _____

_____

sell _____

_____

To Be a Verb

The verb **to be** joins the subject of the sentence with words that describe it. It tells what the subject is or what the condition of the subject is.

I **am** a girl.
I **am** happy.

Circle the form of the verb **to be** in each sentence.

1. My cousin's birthday party is today.

2. He is nine years old.

3. I am nine years old, too.

4. My brother and I are excited.

5. Last year his party was a lot of fun.

Forms of the verb **to be**	
	Present
I	am
he, she, it	is
you, we	are
	Past
I	was
he, she, it	was
you, we	were

Write the correct form of the verb **to be** to complete each sentence.

6. Miss Dawson _____ a teacher.

7. Arnold and Jack _____ brothers.

8. The trip to the zoo _____ a great learning experience.

9. I _____ the oldest child in my family.

10. We _____ on our way out the door when the phone rang.

Using the present and past tense form of the verb **to be**

Verbs That Help

A verb that helps the main verb tell what the subject is doing or did is called a **helping verb.**

We **are** **learning** about animals.

helping verb   main verb

Circle all the helping verbs in each sentence.

1. We were told to research an animal.

2. Each student has selected an animal of interest.

3. I have learned about the tiger's eating habits and habitat.

4. Some students had researched the life cycle of their animal as well.

5. When they were finished they had learned about how the animal defends itself.

Write a helping verb to complete each sentence.

6. Dad _____ taken us to the park.

7. Jeff and I _____ been there before.

8. We _____ seen many interesting animals.

9. After our hike, we ate the lunch we _____ packed.

10. By the time we got home, I _____ fallen asleep!

Words that Describe

A word that describes or tells more about a noun is called an **adjective**. Adjectives can tell how many, what color, and what kind.

We saw **two** **black** birds sitting in the **tall** tree.

Circle all the adjectives in each sentence.

1. The beautiful green grass feels good on my bare feet.

2. The small birdbath is full of chirping robins.

3. The cherry tree has many pretty blossoms.

4. I watch out the window as the swift squirrel gathers nuts and acorns.

5. The misty rain and sparkling sunshine created a vivid rainbow in the cloudless sky.

Write an adjective to complete each sentence.

6. The_____car drove along the _____ road.

7. We saw a_____squirrel in the park.

8. The_____children were amazed by the _____ birds.

9. We hiked along a_____path.

10. The _____ sun shone through the _____ trees.

Using adjectives

Sentence Beginnings and Endings

Every sentence begins with a **capital letter** and ends with a **punctuation mark**.

The party starts at 6:30**.**	A **statement** ends with a period.
What time is it**?**	A **question** ends with a question mark.
Let's go**!**	An **exclamation** ends with an exclamation point.

Read each sentence. Circle the sentences that are written correctly. Rewrite the sentences that are not written correctly.

1. my sister and I went to Lauren's party.

_____

2. We had pizza and it was delicious!

_____

3. Then Lauren opened her presents

_____

4. can you guess what she got

_____

5. lauren's mom gave her a dress.

_____

6. After the gifts were opened, we had cake.

_____

7. the cake was chocolate — my favorite!

_____

8. When we finished our cake, do you know what we played

_____

9. i won a prize for the ring toss game.

_____

10. It was a great party

_____

How Does it End?

Remember: A **statement** ends with a period.
A **question** ends with a question mark.
An **exclamation** ends with an exclamation point.

Read each sentence. Add a period, question mark, or exclamation point to complete it.

1. Where are you going on vacation ___

2. We are going to New York City ___

3. I have never been there before ___

4. New York City is a great place to visit ___

5. I want to see the Statue of Liberty ___

6. Can we climb to the top and look out ___

7. That sounds like so much fun ___

8. What else can we do in New York City ___

9. You can go to Central Park or see a show on Broadway ___

10. I can't wait ___

Write a statement.

_____

Write a question.

_____

Write an exclamation.

_____

Sentences that Run On

A sentence that includes more than one idea is called a **run-on sentence**. To fix a run-on sentence, separate the ideas into individual sentences.

Run-on: My friend has a horse it is black and white.
Corrected: My friend has a horse. It is black and white.

Read each sentence. Circle the sentences that are written correctly. Rewrite the run-on sentences as two separate sentences.

1. Have you seen her new haircut it is much shorter.

_____

2. I am so happy that it is my birthday I can't wait to open my presents.

_____

3. It is not time to go to the store yet we are leaving in ten minutes.

_____

4. Please hang up your clothes and put your toys away.

_____

5. Where were you yesterday did you go to the movie theater?

_____

6. They bought a new car that is red and white.

_____

7. Is mom home yet I need to ask her a question.

_____

8. How long did it take you to make that was it difficult?

_____

9. This game is confusing it doesn't have directions.

_____

10. I'm going to the store do you need anything?

_____

Comma Consistency

Use a **comma** to separate words in a **series** (three or more things).

I packed my **shirt, pants, and socks**.

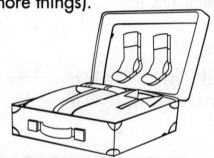

Read each sentence. Add commas where they belong.

1. We went to the beach and took our sunscreen towels shovels and pails.

2. My mom brought strawberries peaches and watermelon for a healthy snack.

3. We played volleyball tossed the frisbee and built a sand castle.

4. The days were fun exciting and tiring!

5. When it was time to go, we shook the sand out of our towels blankets and clothes.

6. On the first day of school, I brought my school supplies book bag and lunch box.

7. We talked about fun activities our daily schedule and what we would learn this year.

8. Our teacher told us to read study math facts and share our thoughts about the first day with our family.

9. I can't wait to learn about multiplication division and fractions!

10. I think school is going to be challenging exciting and fun.

Write a sentence with a series of at least three things.

_____

_____

_____

Make the Comma Connection

Use a **comma** between the name of a city and state and between the day and year.

I live in **Columbus, Ohio**.

We moved here on **July 28, 2001**.

Read each sentence. Add commas where they belong.

1. For vacation, my family went to Orlando Florida.

2. The last time we were there was March 9 2001.

3. We drove through Memphis Tennessee.

4. Our hotel was just outside of Orlando in Kissimmee Florida.

5. We arrived on December 23 2002.

6. We spent a day at the beach in Orlando Florida.

7. Then we spent a day at my aunt and uncle's house in Tampa Florida.

8. Our family celebrated the New Year on January 1 2003.

9. We checked out of the hotel on January 3 2003.

10. On the way home, we visited our grandparents in Atlanta Georgia.

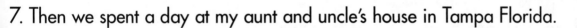

What city and state do you live in?

_____

What day where you born on?

_____

Grammar is Great!

Underline all the nouns and circle all the verbs in each sentence.

1. Our class went on a field trip to the museum.

2. We played games and sang songs on the bus.

3. We arrived at the museum at 10:15.

4. The parent helpers took us around the museum.

5. I enjoyed the field trip to the museum!

Read each sentence. Capitalize each proper noun and add commas where they belong.

6. lucy brown is one of my best friends.

7. We like to play dolls draw pictures and put together puzzles.

8. I invited lucy and maddie over on saturday.

9. we played ate lunch and helped Mrs. johnson with her garden.

10. she planted petunias impatiens and roses.

Write an adjective to describe each noun.

_____ apple   _____ pizza

_____ park   _____ radio

_____ pillow   _____ car

Pudgy's Surprise Visit

Read the story carefully.

Heather had a pet pig named Pudgy. This was the most curious pig you have ever met. One day, Pudgy's curiosity almost got him into big trouble.

It was a beautiful fall morning and the leaves were falling. Heather went out to the pen to feed Pudgy, but to her surprise he was not there. She noticed that the door was wide open and the lock was broken. Trying not to panic, Heather ran back into the house to see if her mom knew where Pudgy was. But Heather's mom had no idea what happened. So Heather went back outside to look for the pig. She looked around the backyard but didn't see him anywhere.

Just then, she heard her mom calling from the back door, "Heather, there is a phone call for you!"

"Great," Heather thought to herself, "I don't have time for this!" But she made her way into the house and picked up the phone. "Hello?"

"Hello, Heather, this is Officer Rich from the police department. Are you missing anything?"

"Pudgy!" Heather shouted in disbelief.

"Yes, Pudgy is just a few doors down here at Mrs. Carson's house and has apparently found a few new friends."

"I'll be right there!" Heather shouted, and with that she hung up the phone and ran to the neighbor's house as quickly as she could.

By the time she got there, Mrs. Carson and Officer Rich were heading for the backyard. Heather followed, and soon she saw Pudgy romping around with Mrs. Carson's four tiny puppies.

Heather immediately apologized to Mrs. Carson and Officer Rich. She promised it would never happen again.

Mrs. Carson laughed and replied, "Not to worry, dear, it was all in good fun!"

Once Heather got back home she asked her dad to help fix the pen so that Pudgy would stay inside it once and for all.

Put it in Order

Think about the story "Pudgy's Surprise Visit."
Number the sentences in the order that they happened
in the story. Reread the story if you need to.

_____ Heather rushed to her mom to tell her
that Pudgy was missing.

_____ Heather went to Mrs. Carson's to get Pudgy.

_____ Pudgy was a curious pig.

_____ Heather went out to feed her pig and he was gone!

_____ Heather asked her dad to help fix the pen so Pudgy would not get out.

_____ Officer Rich called.

_____ Pudgy was romping around in the grass with four tiny puppies.

Do you think Pudgy will make another special visit to his tiny puppy friends?
Why or why not?

_____

_____

_____

_____

What was your favorite part in the story? Describe it.

_____

_____

_____

Remember What You Read

Answer these questions about "Pudgy's Surprise Visit." Reread the story if you need to.

1. What is the main idea of the story?

_____

_____

2. Who are the main characters?

_____

_____

3. How did Heather find out Pudgy was missing?

_____

_____

4. How did Heather end up finding Pudgy?

_____

_____

5. How did Mrs. Carson react to the situation?

_____

_____

6. How did Heather show she was a responsible person?

_____

_____

What Do You Think?

Think about the story "Pudgy's Surprise Visit." Reread the story if you need to.

1. Draw a picture of the look on Heather's face when she found the empty pen.

2. Explain how you think she felt when she saw that Pudgy was not in his pen.

_____

_____

_____

3. Describe what Heather might have done if Officer Rich hadn't called so quickly.

_____

_____

_____

4. What do you think Heather will do differently next time?

_____

_____

_____

Making predictions

Be Persuasive

Writing that states an opinion with supporting reasons is called **persuasive writing**. Its purpose is to convince someone else to agree with your opinion.

Begin with a **topic sentence** that clearly states your opinion. This sentence needs to capture your audience's attention. To convince them to continue reading. The next several sentences include **reasons that support your opinion**. They must be well thought out and clearly stated. Remember, you are trying to persuade your audience with reasons that are important to them. Finally, end with a **conclusion**. This should remind your audience about your opinion and why they should agree.

Read the paragraph carefully.

Our class should collect toys for the Children's Hospital. There are several important reasons why we should donate toys to this cause. One reason is because children at the hospital do not have toys and games to play with. Also, many of us have toys that we do not play with anymore. These toys just sit at the bottom of our toy boxes when they could be used by children at the hospital. Another important reason is that the hospital does not have the money to buy toys and games for the children who are staying there. We can help! It certainly is no fun being in the hospital, and our used toys and games could cheer up the children as they recover! To make it easier for our parents, a truck could come and pick up our donations at school. Let's donate our used toys and games for the children in the hospital who need them. Think about how good you will feel knowing you helped someone!

1. Do you feel the author of the paragraph above was persuasive? Why or why not?

_____

_____

2. Why is persuasive writing important?

_____

3. What would you like to persuade someone to do? Write a topic sentence and at least two reasons.

_____

_____

Express Yourself in a Poem

Haiku is an ancient form of poetry that was created in Japan centuries ago. Haiku poems are mostly written about the beauty of nature. The form that this type of poetry follows is simple. It usually has three lines: the first with five syllables, the second with seven syllables, and the third with five syllables.

Line 1:	a deep blue ocean	(5 syllables)
Line 2:	a little fish was swimming	(7 syllables)
Line 3:	trying to find food	(5 syllables)

Write your own Haiku.

_____

_____

_____

Another fun kind of poem to write is the **Why Poem**. A Why Poem is written about things the writer wonders about but does not know the answers to. It ends with an explanation of something the writer understands very well.

Read the poem.

I don't understand
Why some people are homeless
Why there are people without food
Why there is violence in the world
But I really don't understand
Why people can be unkind

What I understand the most is that
My family loves me and is proud of me
Because I always do my best

Write your own Why Poem.

_____

_____

_____

_____

_____

_____

_____

_____

_____

_____

_____

Writing poetry

You May Not Know It, But You Can be a Poet!

Poetry can rhyme. When every two lines rhyme, they are called **couplets**.

My Family

Mom, your stories touch my day with laughter and a smile.
I appreciate your warmth and ever-loving style.

Billy, your gentleness adds a special touch to my day,
And your giving heart shows more to me than words could ever say.

Sara, your caring and sensitive side is special about you.
These qualities you hold will help in everything that you do.

Dad, you are a special friend with hugs for me each day.
You brighten up my life in such a fantastic way.

Write your own poem with couplets.

_____

_____

_____

_____

_____

_____

_____

_____

_____

_____

_____

_____

_____

Consonant Digraphs

Say each word. Circle the consonant digraph in each word.

chips	shell	then	wheel
fish	when	cherry	booth
with	chow	ship	why

Underline the consonant digraph in each word. Then write a sentence using the word.

charity_____

friendship_____

theater_____

whine_____

wish_____

Write the missing consonant digraph to complete each word. Then rewrite the word.

___ ___ i l e _____

___ ___ a l l e n g e _____

___ ___ i n e _____

___ ___ a l l o w _____

___ ___ r e a d _____

Reviewing consonant digraphs

Prefixes and Suffixes

Add a prefix or suffix to complete each word in the sentences.

1. I went to the gas station to _____fill my gas tank.

2. After I put lotion on my hands they were much soft_____.

3. When you say thank you, you are showing people
   that you are respect_____.

prefixes	suffixes
un	er
re	est
pre	ful
	less

4. The frown on his face told us that he was _____happy.

5. We took a _____test to see how much we knew before we started the chapter.

6. When you are still and not moving, you are motion_____.

7. One of the great_____ feelings is when someone shows they care about you.

8. She has good foot skills, which make her an excellent soccer play_____.

Write a sentence using each word.

wonderful _____

_____

remake _____

_____

taller _____

_____

unsure _____

_____

Synonyms and Antonyms

Write a synonym and antonym for each underlined word.

1. On the last day of school, our class was very <u>sad</u>.

Synonym:_____ Antonym:_____

2. We went to the park and had a <u>good</u> time.

Synonym:_____ Antonym:_____

3. My mother makes the <u>best</u> chocolate cake.

Synonym:_____ Antonym:_____

4. Sally turned down the volume on the television because she said it was too <u>loud</u>.

Synonym:_____ Antonym:_____

5. I was <u>glad</u> to be done with that project.

Synonym:_____ Antonym:_____

6. The rainbow was <u>beautiful</u> and colorful.

Synonym:_____ Antonym:_____

7. When he received the ribbon he looked very <u>excited</u>.

Synonym:_____ Antonym:_____

8. I thanked my mom in a <u>quiet</u> voice.

Synonym:_____ Antonym:_____

9. The bear was big and <u>scary</u>.

Synonym:_____ Antonym:_____

10. After the game, the players were <u>tired</u>.

Synonym:_____ Antonym:_____

Main Idea and Details

Write the main idea and
supporting details for each paragraph.

There are three main differences between butterflies
and moths. First, butterflies are usually brightly colored and moths
are usually dull in color. Second, butterflies are active during the day
and moths are active at night. Third, butterflies form a chrysalis and
moths form a cocoon.

Main idea _____

_____

Supporting details _____

_____

_____

Toads and frogs have many differences. One
difference is their skin. A toad's skin is warty and dry, but
the skin of a frog is moist and smooth. Also, toads tend to
walk, while frogs tend to jump. And toads and frogs have
different-looking feet. Toads have almost no webbing on
their feet, but frog feet are usually fully webbed. Another major
difference is where they live. Toads typically live on land and away
from water. Frogs, on the other hand, live in or near water.

Main idea _____

_____

Supporting details _____

_____

_____

Descriptive Writing

Think about a special time that you shared with a family member, such as going fishing with Grandpa, going swimming with Mom, or planting flowers with an aunt. Write your special moment on the line.

My special moment is:

_____

Write some details about your special moment in the box.

_____

Write a paragraph about your special moment using the supporting details.

_____

_____

_____

_____

_____

_____

_____

Writing a descriptive paragraph

Complete Sentences

Rewrite each group of words to make complete sentences.

1. the playground went to I

_____

2. My aunt at the clothing store works

_____

3. monkey on the swing Do you see the

_____

4. movie Lynn and I on Saturday saw a

_____

5. two big dogs next live door

_____

6. My favorite checkers game is

_____

7. driving a red bird saw my father while to work

_____

8. got wet socks my

_____

9. We decided to baseball play

_____

10. home for a snack I came

_____

Run-on Sentences

Read each run-on sentence. Rewrite it as two separate sentences.

1. I like to play baseball I am on a team.

_____

2. We went to the field the game was cancelled because of rain.

_____

3. John was sad he wanted to try out his new baseball glove.

_____

4. We left the field Dad asked if we wanted to stop for ice cream.

_____

5. That surprised us we got to order a sundae or a cone.

_____

6. I ordered a double scoop of chocolate Dad ordered vanilla.

_____

7. We had fun we ate at a picnic table.

_____

8. It was time to go we thanked Dad!

_____

9. Dad said, "You're welcome" he enjoyed it, too.

_____

10. On the way home, we talked about baseball we talked about basketball, too.

_____

Subjects and Predicates

Read each sentence. Circle the subject and underline the predicate.

1. Our family goes on a vacation every year.

2. The best vacation was when we went to Washington, D.C.

3. We saw so many historic sights.

4. My favorite part was the tour of the White House.

Add a subject to complete each sentence.

5. _____ went to the library.

6. _____ and I ride bicycles together.

7. _____ was late getting to work yesterday.

8. _____ sells three flavors of ice cream.

Add a predicate to complete each sentence.

9. The man_____.

10. Jerry and Jason _____.

11. Natalie_____.

12. The boat _____.

Three Parts of Speech

Read each sentence. Circle the nouns. Draw a box around the verbs.

1. Yesterday we helped with yard work.

2. I pulled weeds in the flowerbeds.

3. Jackie and Mom planted flowers.

4. Dad and Leslie got the dirt in the garden ready.

5. The clouds grew dark but it didn't rain.

6. We had fun helping each other!

Read each sentence. Underline the adjectives.

7. The little girl ate an enormous slice of pizza.

8. She rode her shiny, new bike to the park.

9. The brightly-colored sailboat drifted smoothly across the water.

10. My grandma and I made delicious homemade brownies.

11. The beautiful sunset was a sight to behold.

12. The drive was fun and exciting.

Pronouns

Read each sentence. Circle all the pronouns.

1. We made pizza for dinner.

2. It tasted really good.

3. We added many ingredients to the pizza.

4. I wanted to put pepperoni on it.

5. Rick wanted to put extra cheese on it.

6. He also wanted sausage, but we didn't have any.

7. Dad said that he had a taste for mushrooms.

8. It was the best pizza I ever tasted.

9. Maybe we should open our own pizza shop.

10. It would probably be a lot of fun!

Write a pronoun that can take the place of the underlined nouns.

11. _____ Rick and I had fun making pizza.

12. _____ Dad helped us make the pizza.

13. _____ Dad had lots of fun, too.

14. _____ My mom and sister asked for a slice.

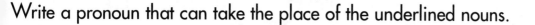

15. _____ My sister didn't like the mushrooms.

Capitals and Punctuation

Read the sentences. Rewrite them using capital letters and punctuation.

1. yesterday we went to the swimming pool

_____

2. jeff and i got really tired from swimming a lot

_____

3. do you know what i like best about the day

_____

4. i loved the water slide

_____

5. sometimes the line for the slide was long

_____

6. ashly can dive very well

_____

7. did you see ashly dive

_____

8. mom brought healthy snacks for us to eat

_____

9. the snacks helped give us energy

_____

10. we all had so much fun

_____

Commas

Read each sentence. Add commas where they belong.

1. For my birthday, I am having a party with my family friends and neighbors.

2. I invited Ian Adam and Eric.

3. Robbie Joseph and Noah are coming, too.

4. We are going to play volleyball have a water balloon toss and go swimming.

5. You need to take your time throw carefully and concentrate during the balloon toss.

6. For lunch we are having hamburgers cheeseburgers and hotdogs.

7. I love cheeseburgers with ketchup mustard and pickles.

8. Dad likes his with lettuce onions and tomatoes, too.

9. We also are having potato salad baked beans and pasta salad.

10. Dessert is a sundae with strawberry chocolate and vanilla ice cream!

11. I am looking forward to opening my gifts and playing with my friends.

12. Aunt Betty Aunt Rose and Uncle Len each brought a present for me.

13. One present is from Mom Dad and Bobby.

14. I am really hoping to get a new bike a helmet and a raft for the pool.

15. Parties are great because family friends and neighbors get to visit with each other!

Sugar and Spice

Read the story carefully.

Once a week, Michelle and Ryan stop by the pet shop on their way home from school. They mainly stop for two reasons—Sugar and Spice. Sugar and Spice are two kittens that share a cage. They play so nicely together. Michelle and Ryan both have been begging their parents for a kitten for weeks. Since they are neighbors, they thought it would be perfect if Michelle got Sugar and Ryan got Spice.

Things got busy at school and home, so Michelle and Ryan didn't have time to stop by the pet shop. How they missed seeing Sugar and Spice. A few weeks later, Michelle and her mom passed by the pet shop when they were out. To Michelle's surprise, she didn't see Spice in the front window; she only saw Sugar. A terrible thought crossed her mind—someone bought Spice and the two best friends would never be together again. She went home practically in tears, but her mom assured her everything would be okay.

That weekend was Ryan's birthday party. Michelle was really looking forward to going because Ryan's parties were always fun. At the party, they played games, sang, and ate cake and ice cream. Then came the best part—the presents! Ryan got lots of neat toys, including a few that Michelle was planning to put on her own birthday list. Just when Ryan thought he was done opening all the presents, his dad brought out a small box with holes in it and a bow on top. Ryan carefully opened the box and found Spice inside!

Ryan had mixed feelings. He was excited to have a new kitten, but he was also sad that Spice was not with his best friend Sugar anymore. Ryan's parents sensed his sad feeling and motioned for Michelle's mom, who stepped forward with a small box with holes in it and a bow on top. The box looked just like the one that Ryan got. Michelle's mom asked Michelle if she wanted an early birthday present. But before Michelle could answer, Ryan had the box open and Sugar was peeking out! Sugar and Spice immediately started playing together and Ryan looked at Michelle and said, "This is the best birthday ever!"

Reading

Story Details and Sequence

Think about the story "Sugar and Spice."
Number the sentences in the order that they happened
in the story. Reread the story if you need to.

_____Michelle got Sugar as an early birthday present.

_____Michelle and Ryan stopped by the pet shop once a week.

_____Michelle went to Ryan's birthday party.

_____Michelle and Ryan got busy at school and home and could not stop by
the pet shop.

_____Ryan opened his last present. It was Spice!

_____Michelle and her mom passed by the pet shop and saw that Spice was not there.

Do you think Sugar and Spice will continue to be best friends? Why or why not?

_____

_____

_____

_____

What was your favorite part in the story? Describe it.

_____

_____

_____

_____

What Do You Remember?

Answer these questions about "Sugar and Spice." Reread the story if you need to.

1. What is the main idea of the story?

_____

_____

2. Who are the main characters?

_____

3. How did Michelle and Ryan feel about Sugar and Spice?

_____

_____

_____

4. Why did Michelle and Ryan stop going to the pet shop after school?

_____

_____

_____

5. How did Michelle react when she and her mom did not see Spice at the pet shop?

_____

_____

_____

6. How do you think Michelle and Ryan feel about their new kittens?

_____

_____

Predict the Outcome

Think about the story "Sugar and Spice." Reread the story if you need to.

1. Draw a picture of the look on Ryan's and Michelle's faces when they opened their presents and saw Sugar and Spice.

2. Explain how you think they felt when they saw Sugar and Spice together again.

_____

_____

_____

3. Describe how you think Ryan's feelings changed after Michelle opened her early birthday present.

_____

_____

_____

4. Who do you think is happier, Ryan and Michelle or Sugar and Spice? Why?

_____

_____

_____

Persuasive Writing

1. List some ideas of things that you would like to persuade someone to do.

- _____   - _____

- _____   - _____

- _____   - _____

- _____   - _____

2. Choose one idea and write a persuasive letter.

Dear_____ ,

    I think you should _____.

There are several reasons why this is a good idea. One reason is _____

_____.

Another reason is _____

_____.

Finally, _____

_____.

Just think about how good you will feel_____

_____.

Sincerely,

_____

Answer Key

Please take time to review the work your child has completed and remember to praise both success and effort. If your child makes a mistake, let him or her know that mistakes are a part of learning. Then explain the correct answer and how to find it. Taking the time to help your child and an active interest in his or her progress shows that you feel learning is important.

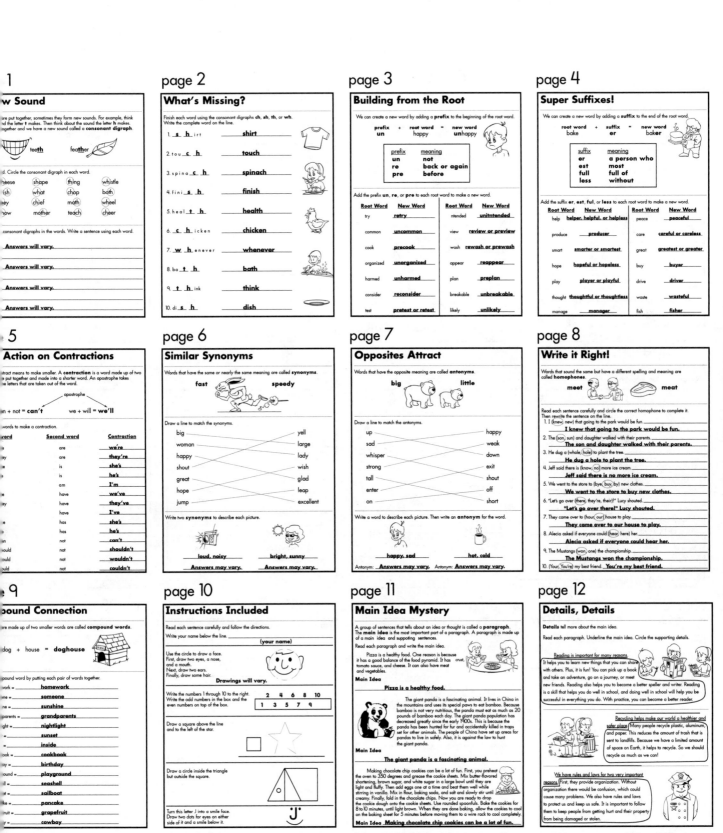

page 1

New Sound

...are put together, sometimes they form new sounds. For example, think ...nd the letter **t** makes. Then think about the sound the letter **h** makes. ...ogether and we have a new sound called a **consonant digraph**.

tee**th**   fea**th**er

...d. Circle the consonant digraph in each word.

...heese	shape	thing	whistle
...ish	what	chop	both
...ey	chief	math	wheel
...how	mother	teach	cheer

...consonant digraphs in the words. Write a sentence using each word.

Answers will vary.

Answers will vary.

Answers will vary.

Answers will vary.

page 2

What's Missing?

Finish each word using the consonant digraphs **ch, sh, th,** or **wh**.
Write the complete word on the line.

1. **s h** irt — shirt
2. tou **c h** — touch
3. spina **c h** — spinach
4. fini **s h** — finish
5. heal **t h** — health
6. **c h** icken — chicken
7. **w h** enever — whenever
8. ba **t h** — bath
9. **t h** ink — think
10. di **s h** — dish

page 3

Building from the Root

We can create a new word by adding a **prefix** to the beginning of the root word.

prefix + **root word** = **new word**
un + happy = unhappy

prefix	meaning
un	not
re	back or again
pre	before

Add the prefix **un**, **re**, or **pre** to each root word to make a new word.

Root Word	New Word	Root Word	New Word
try	retry	ntended	unintended
common	uncommon	view	review or preview
cook	precook	wash	rewash or prewash
organized	unorganized	appear	reappear
harmed	unharmed	plan	preplan
consider	reconsider	breakable	unbreakable
test	pretest or retest	likely	unlikely

page 4

Super Suffixes!

We can create a new word by adding a **suffix** to the end of the root word.

root word + **suffix** = **new word**
bake + er = baker

suffix	meaning
er	a person who
est	most
full	full of
less	without

Add the suffix **er, est, ful,** or **less** to each root word to make a new word.

Root Word	New Word	Root Word	New Word
help	helper, helpful, or helpless	peace	peaceful
produce	producer	care	careful or careless
smart	smarter or smartest	great	greatest or greater
hope	hopeful or hopeless	buy	buyer
play	player or playful	drive	driver
thought	thoughtful or thoughtless	waste	wasteful
manage	manager	fish	fisher

page 5

Action on Contractions

...tract means to make smaller. A **contraction** is a word made up of two ... put together and made into a shorter word. An apostrophe takes ...e letters that are taken out of the word.

apostrophe
...n + not = **can't**   we + will = **we'll**

...words to make a contraction.

...ord	Second word	Contraction
...e	are	we're
...ey	are	they're
...e	is	she's
...e	is	he's
...e	am	I'm
...e	have	we've
...ey	have	they've
...e	have	I've
...e	has	she's
...e	has	he's
...e	not	can't
...ould	not	shouldn't
...ould	not	wouldn't
...ould	not	couldn't

page 6

Similar Synonyms

Words that have the same or nearly the same meaning are called **synonyms**.

fast   speedy

Draw a line to match the synonyms.

big — large
woman — lady
happy — glad
shout — yell
great — excellent
hope — wish
jump — leap

Write two **synonyms** to describe each picture.

loud, noisy   bright, sunny
Answers may vary.   Answers may vary.

page 7

Opposites Attract

Words that have the opposite meaning are called **antonyms**.

big   little

Draw a line to match the antonyms.

up — down
sad — happy
whisper — shout
strong — weak
tall — short
enter — exit
on — off

Write a word to describe each picture. Then write an **antonym** for the word.

happy, sad   hot, cold
Antonym: Answers may vary.   Antonym: Answers may vary.

page 8

Write it Right!

Words that sound the same but have a different spelling and meaning are called **homophones**.

meet   meat

Read each sentence carefully and circle the correct homophone to complete it. Then rewrite the sentence on the line.

1. I (knew, new) that going to the park would be fun.
   I knew that going to the park would be fun.
2. The (son, sun) and daughter walked with their parents.
   The son and daughter walked with their parents.
3. He dug a (whole, hole) to plant the tree.
   He dug a hole to plant the tree.
4. Jeff said there is (know, no) more ice cream.
   Jeff said there is no more ice cream.
5. We went to the store to (buy, by) new clothes.
   We want to the store to buy new clothes.
6. "Let's go over (there, they're, their)!" Lucy shouted.
   "Let's go over there!" Lucy shouted.
7. They came over to (our, hour) house to play.
   They came over to our house to play.
8. Alecia asked if everyone could (hear, here) her.
   Alecia asked if everyone could hear her.
9. The Mustangs (won, one) the championship.
   The Mustangs won the championship.
10. (Your, You're) my best friend. **You're my best friend.**

page 9

Compound Connection

...re made up of two smaller words are called **compound words**.

dog + house = **doghouse**

...pound word by putting each pair of words together.

...work = homework
...ne = someone
...ine = sunshine
...parents = grandparents
...ght = nightlight
... = sunset
... = inside
...ook = cookbook
...ay = playground
...ll = seashell
... = sailboat
... = pancake
...ruit = grapefruit
... = cowboy

page 10

Instructions Included

Read each sentence carefully and follow the directions.

Write your name below the line.

(your name)

Use the circle to draw a face.
First, draw two eyes, a nose, and a mouth.
Next, draw two ears.
Finally, draw some hair.

Drawings will vary.

Write the numbers 1 through 10 to the right.
Write the odd numbers in the box and the even numbers on top of the box.

2 4 6 8 10
1 3 5 7 9

Draw a square above the line and to the left of the star.

Draw a circle inside the triangle but outside the square.

Turn this letter J into a smile face.
Draw two dots for eyes on either side of it and a smile below it.

page 11

Main Idea Mystery

A group of sentences that tells about an idea or thought is called a **paragraph**. The **main idea** is the most important part of a paragraph. A paragraph is made up of a main idea and supporting sentences.

Read each paragraph and write the main idea.

Pizza is a healthy food. One reason is because it has a good balance of the food pyramid. It has crust, tomato sauce, and cheese. It can also have meat and vegetables.

Main Idea
Pizza is a healthy food.

The giant panda is a fascinating animal. It lives in China in the mountains and uses its special paws to eat bamboo. Because bamboo is not very nutritious, the panda must eat as much as 20 pounds of bamboo each day. The giant panda population has decreased greatly since the early 1900s. This is because the panda has been hunted for fur and accidentally killed in traps set for other animals. The people of China have set up areas for pandas to live in safely. Also, it is against the law to hunt the giant panda.

Main Idea
The giant panda is a fascinating animal.

Making chocolate chip cookies can be a lot of fun. First, you preheat the oven to 350 degrees and grease the cookie sheets. Mix butter-flavored shortening, brown sugar, and white sugar in a large bowl until they are light and fluffy. Then add eggs one at a time and beat them while stirring in vanilla. Mix in flour, baking soda, and salt and slowly stir until creamy. Finally, fold in the chocolate chips. When they are done baking, allow the cookies to cool on the baking sheet for 5 minutes before moving them to a wire rack to cool completely.

Main Idea **Making chocolate chip cookies can be a lot of fun.**

page 12

Details, Details

Details tell more about the main idea.

Read each paragraph. Underline the main idea. Circle the supporting details.

Reading is important for many reasons. It helps you to learn new things that you can share with others. Plus, it is fun! You can pick up a book and take an adventure, go on a journey, or meet new friends. Reading also helps you to become a better speller and writer. Reading is a skill that helps you do well in school, and doing well in school will help you be successful in everything you do. With practice, you can become a better reader.

Recycling helps make our world a healthier and safer place. Many people recycle plastic, aluminum, and paper. This reduces the amount of trash that is sent to landfills. Because we have a limited amount of space on Earth, it helps to recycle. So we should recycle as much as we can!

We have rules and laws for two very important reasons. First, they provide organization. Without organization there would be confusion, which could cause many problems. We also have rules and laws to protect us and keep us safe. It is important to follow them to keep people from getting hurt and their property from being damaged or stolen.

page 13

Super Supporting Details

Read each main idea. Write two or three sentences with details that support the main idea.

Eating healthy food is important for many reasons. **Your body needs nutrition. It helps you grow and stay healthy. Your body turns the food into energy. You do better in school.**
(Answers will vary.)

It is important for children to get about nine or ten hours of sleep every night.
Your body needs rest. It helps you stay healthy.
You can think more clearly.
You do better in school.
(Answers will vary.)

Throwing away your trash at the park is important for many reasons.
It keeps the park looking good.
It is healthy for those who visit.
It keeps the plants and animals safe.
(Answers will vary.)

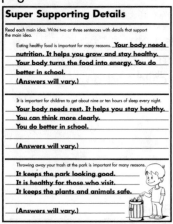

page 14

Describe It!

Think of a topic that you are interested in. It could be a hobby, an animal, or a person. Write your topic in the main idea circle. Then write four facts about your topic in the detail boxes.

Detail | Detail | Main Idea | Detail | Detail

(Answers will vary.)

Write a paragraph using your main topic and supporting details.

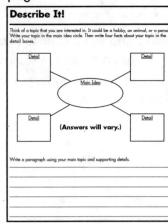

page 15

You Be the Writer

Select a topic from the box below and write it in the main idea circle. Then write four facts about your topic in the detail boxes.

Topics	
sports	pets
grandparents	animals at the zoo
sister or brother	hobbies

Detail | Detail | Main Idea | Detail | Detail

(Answers will vary.)

Write a paragraph using your main topic and supporting details.

page 16

What's in a Sentence?

A sentence must begin with a capital letter and end with a period (.), exclama… (!), or question mark (?). Also, every sentence must have a **naming part** … an **action part**. The naming part tells who or what the sentence is about. T… part tells what the naming part does or is.

capital letter → **The dogs** **bark.** ← period
naming part / action part

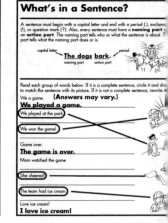

Read each group of words below. If it is a complete sentence, circle it and dr… to match the sentence with its picture. If it is not a complete sentence, rewrite it…

We a game. **(Answers may vary.)**
We played a game.
We played at the park.
We won the game!
Game over.
The game is over.
Mom watched the game
She cheered!
The team had ice cream.
Love ice cream!
I love ice cream!

page 17

Making Sentences Complete

Rewrite each group of words to make it a complete sentence.

1. lena went to the store to buy flowers
Lena went to the store to buy flowers.
2. ben his mom if they could go to the store.
Ben asked his mom if they could go to the store.
3. Lauren and her brother played in the yard
Lauren and her brother played in the yard.
4. is teaching her how to knit.
Her mom is teaching her how to knit.
5. grandpa woke up early to go fishing.
Grandpa woke up early to go fishing.

Write complete sentences using the words in the box. Only use each word or group of words once. **Answers may vary.**

went to the library	took a boat to the island	Gary and Michelle	Shelly and I
played in the clubhouse	stood in line for an hour	Jonathan	We
skated to my house		The whole class	

6. **Shelly and I went to the library.**
7. **Gary and Michelle played in the clubhouse.**
8. **Jonathan skated to my house.**
9. **The whole class took a boat to the island.**
10. **We stood in line for an hour.**

page 18

It Takes Two

Every sentence has two main parts. The naming part, or the part that tells who the sentence is about, is called the **subject**. The action part, or the part that tells what the subject does or is, is called the **predicate**.

Lions **roar.**
subject predicate

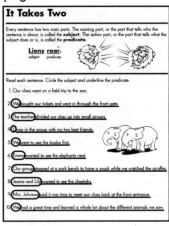

Read each sentence. Circle the subject and underline the predicate.

1. Our class went on a field trip to the zoo.
2. We bought our tickets and went in through the front gate.
3. The teacher divided our class up into small groups.
4. I was in the group with my two best friends.
5. We went to see the koalas first.
6. Emma wanted to see the elephants next.
7. Our group stopped at a park bench to have a snack while we watched the giraffes.
8. Jeanie and Lily wanted to see the cheetahs.
9. Mrs. Johnson said it was time to meet our class back at the front entrance.
10. We had a great time and learned a whole lot about the different animals we saw.

page 19

Spectacular Subjects

Write a subject from the list to complete each sentence. Use each subject only once.

The truck	*The Smiths*
We	*Alexis and Karen*
Grandma and grandpa	*Ashley*
The pet shop	*Jack and Alan*
Our class	*The team*

(Answers may vary.)

1. **Ashley** walked home from school today.
2. **Jack and Alan** are on the same baseball team.
3. **Our class** earned an extra recess for excellent behavior.
4. **The truck** brought all the furniture to their new house.
5. **The pet shop** has practically every species of fish!
6. **Alexis and Karen** played outside all day.
7. **The Smiths** built a new clubhouse in their backyard.
8. **We** ordered a new red car.
9. **The team** thought they played their best game yet.
10. **Grandma and Grandpa** watched a movie on Saturday afternoon.

page 20

Powerful Predicates **Answer may v…**

Write a predicate from the list to complete each sentence. Use each predicate …

went to the playground with her babysitter.
broke when my brother threw it on the floor.
planted a colorful bush in their garden.
was having a huge sale.
had fun at the parade.
enjoyed the beautiful sunshine today.
was playing my favorite song.
is a healthy snack.
was very relaxing.
went to the pool for the day.

(Answers may vary.)

1. They **planted a colorful bush in their garden.**
2. The toy **broke when my brother threw it to the …**
3. We **enjoyed the beautiful sunshine today.**
4. The radio **was playing my favorite song.**
5. My family **had fun at the parade.**
6. Jessica **went to the playground with her babysi…**
7. An apple **is a healthy snack.**
8. The vacation **was very relaxing.**
9. The store **was having a huge sale.**
10. Their friends **went to the pool for the day.**

page 21

Know Your Nouns

A **noun** is a person, place, or thing.

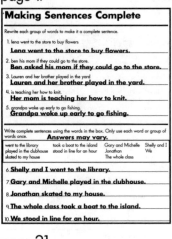

Circle all the nouns in each sentence.

1. Mr. Green planted a vegetable garden last weekend.
2. The garden is filled with lettuce and tomatoes.
3. Broccoli and carrots are growing, too.
4. Mr. Green waters the garden every day.
5. My mother asked Mr. Green for some tomatoes.
6. The bunnies in the neighborhood like the carrots.
7. Mr. Green put up a fence to keep the bunnies out.
8. One bunny squeezed under the fence.
9. The bunny ate two carrots.
10. Mr. Green chased the bunny out of the garden.

page 22

Proper Noun Town

A **proper noun** names a specific person, place, or thing. Proper nouns always begin with a capital letter.

Mr. Green

Circle all the proper nouns in each sentence.

1. Where does your Grandma Shirley live?
2. She lives in Pittsburgh, Pennsylvania.
3. Her house is on Oak Street.
4. Every year the Wilson family goes to Florida.
5. They have lots of fun swimming in the Atlantic Ocean.
6. David turns ten this year.
7. His birthday is in July.
8. David wants to go to Midtown Bowling for his birthday.

Think of a proper noun for each noun. Write it on the line. **Answers will vary.**

a person ______ a month ______
a city ______ a team ______
a library ______ a game ______
a book ______ a store ______
a teacher ______ a restaurant ______

page 23

Two or More

A noun that names more than one person, place, or thing is called a **plural noun**.

There are four different ways to make a noun plural.

For most nouns, add **s**		For nouns that end in **x, z, ch,** or **sh,** add **es**	
hat	hats	box	boxes
For nouns that end with a consonant **y** pattern, change the **y** to **i** and add **es**		Irregular plural	
party	parties	child	children

Look at the ending of each noun. Make the noun plural and write it on the line.

computer	**computers**	box	**boxes**
book	**books**	ditch	**ditches**
watch	**watches**	puppy	**puppies**
goose	**geese**	table	**tables**
candy	**candies**	swing	**swings**
boat	**boats**	dish	**dishes**
lily	**lilies**	freeze	**freezes**
fox	**foxes**	itch	**itches**
wish	**wishes**	door	**doors**
sandwich	**sandwiches**	light	**lights**
tree	**trees**	clubhouse	**clubhouses**

page 24

Get Personal with Pronouns

Pronouns are words that take the place of nouns.

(She)
Emily gave the books to Alex.

She gave the books to Alex.

Pronouns
I he she we they it you

Read the sentences. Underline the nouns and circle the pronouns.

1. The sunset was a shade of pinkish orange. It was beautiful.
2. The sky was clear. It was blue.
3. The sailboats drifted on the water. They moved quickly.
4. Johnny wanted to go on the boat. Mom said it wasn't safe.
5. Johnny stayed at home. He played with Billy.
6. Sam caught a fish. It was pretty big.
7. Sam struggled with the fish. Mom watched him.
8. Dad and Sam put the fish in a bucket. They brought it home.
9. The fish had a funny smell. It wasn't good.
10. Mom cooked the fish. Then Dad and Sam ate it.

page 25

Subject Switch

Some pronouns take the place of nouns in the subject of the sentence.

Lucy rode her bike to school.
She rode her bike to school.

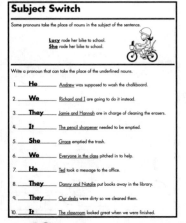

Write a pronoun that can take the place of the underlined nouns.

1. **He** Andrew was supposed to wash the chalkboard.
2. **We** Richard and I are going to do it instead.
3. **They** Jamie and Hannah are in charge of cleaning the erasers.
4. **It** The pencil sharpener needed to be emptied.
5. **She** Grace emptied the trash.
6. **We** Everyone in the class pitched in to help.
7. **He** Ted took a message to the office.
8. **They** Danny and Natalie put books away in the library.
9. **They** Our desks were dirty so we cleaned them.
10. **It** The classroom looked great when we were finished.

page 26

Trading Nouns for Pronouns

Some pronouns take the place of nouns that come after a verb.

The bus driver gave the students a treat on the last day of school.

The bus driver gave **them** a treat on the last day of school.

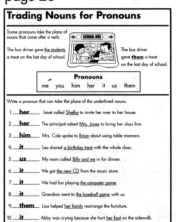

Pronouns
me you him her it us them

Write a pronoun that can take the place of the underlined nouns.

1. **her** Janet called Shelby to invite her over to her house.
2. **her** The principal asked Mrs. Jones to bring her class first.
3. **him** Mrs. Cole spoke to Brian about using table manners.
4. **it** Leo shared a birthday treat with the whole class.
5. **us** My mom called Billy and me in for dinner.
6. **it** We got the new CD from the music store.
7. **it** We had fun playing the computer game.
8. **it** Grandma went to the baseball game with us.
9. **them** Lisa helped her family rearrange the furniture.
10. **it** Abby was crying because she hurt her foot on the sidewalk.

page 27

Take Action with Verbs

A **verb** tells what a person or thing does.

The gorilla **pounds** on its chest.

Circle all the verbs in each sentence.

1. The grizzly bear sneaked into the cave.
2. We watched the koala climb the tree with ease.
3. The parrot flew from one tree to another.
4. The zookeeper fed the elephants.
5. The monkeys acted silly when they saw us watching them!
6. The seals glided through the water quickly.
7. The cheetah ran as fast as lightning.
8. We learned that the kangaroo uses its tail for balance.
9. The penguins slid on the ice.
10. The lion roared at us!

Write a sentence using each verb.

reach **Answers will vary.**

sell **Answers will vary.**

page 28

To Be a Verb

The verb **to be** joins the subject of the sentence with words that describe it. It… what the subject is or what the condition of the subject is.

I **am** a girl.
I **am** happy.

Circle the form of the verb **to be** in each sentence.

1. My cousin's birthday party is today.
2. He is nine years old.
3. I am nine years old, too.
4. My brother and I are excited.
5. Last year his party was a lot of fun.

Forms of the verb to…	
	Prese…
I	am
he, she, it	is
you, we	are
	Pas…
I	was
he, she, it	was
you, we	wer…

Write the correct form of the verb **to be** to complete each sentence.

6. Miss Dawson **is** a teacher.
7. Arnold and Jack **are** brothers.
8. The trip to the zoo **was** a great learning experience.
9. I **am** the oldest child in my family.
10. We **were** on our way out the door when the phone rang.

e 29

s That Help

helps the main verb tell what the subject is doing or did is called ...verb.

We **are** **learning** about animals.

helping verb   main verb

...helping verbs in each sentence.

...old to research an animal.

...dents has selected an animal of interest.

...arned about the tiger's eating habits and habitat.

...dents had researched the life cycle of their animal as well.

...ey were finished they had learned about how the animal defends itself.

is

...ing verb to complete each sentence.

has taken us to the park.

have been there before.

ave seen many interesting animals.

...hike, we ate the lunch we **had** packed.

...ne we got home, I **had** fallen asleep!

page 30

Words that Describe

A word that describes or tells more about a noun is called an **adjective**. Adjectives can tell how many, what color, and what kind.

We saw **two** **black** birds sitting in the **tall** tree.

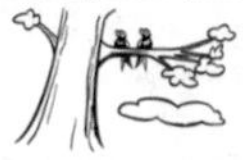

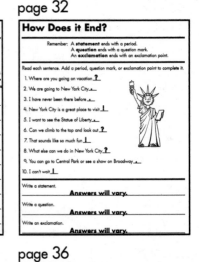

Circle all the adjectives in each sentence.

1. The beautiful green grass feels good on my bare feet.
2. The small birdbath is full of chirping robins.
3. The cherry tree has many pretty blossoms.
4. I watch out the window as the swift squirrel gathers nuts and acorns.
5. The misty rain and sparkling sunshine created a vivid rainbow in the cloudless sky.

Write an adjective to complete each sentence. **(Answers may vary.)**

6. The **fast** car drove along the **long** road.
7. We saw a **brown** squirrel in the park.
8. The **three** children were amazed by the **little** birds.
9. We hiked along a **narrow** path.
10. The **bright** sun shone through the **tall** trees.

page 31

Sentence Beginnings and Endings

Every sentence begins with a **capital letter** and ends with a **punctuation mark**.

The party starts at 6:30. — A **statement** ends with a period.

What time is it? — A **question** ends with a question mark.

Let's go! — An **exclamation** ends with an exclamation point.

Read each sentence. Circle the sentences that are written correctly. Rewrite the sentences that are not written correctly.

1. my sister and I went to Lauren's party.
   My sister and I went to Lauren's party.
2. We had pizza and it was delicious!
3. Then Lauren opened her presents
   Then Lauren opened her presents.
4. can you guess what she got
   Can you guess what she got?
5. lauren's mom gave her a dress.
   Lauren's mom gave her a dress.
6. After the gifts were opened, we had cake.
7. the cake was chocolate—my favorite!
   The cake was chocolate—my favorite!
8. When we finished our cake, do you know what we played
   When we finished our cake, do you know what we played?
9. i won a prize for the ring toss game.
   I won a prize for the ring toss game.
10. It was a great party **It was a great party!**

page 32

How Does it End?

Remember: A **statement** ends with a period.
A **question** ends with a question mark.
An **exclamation** ends with an exclamation point.

Read each sentence. Add a period, question mark, or exclamation point to complete it.

1. Where are you going on vacation **?**
2. We are going to New York City **.**
3. I have never been there before **.**
4. New York City is a great place to visit **!**
5. I want to see the Statue of Liberty **.**
6. Can we climb to the top and look out **?**
7. That sounds like so much fun **!**
8. What else can we do in New York City **?**
9. You can go to Central Park or see a show on Broadway **.**
10. I can't wait **!**

Write a statement.
Answers will vary.

Write a question.
Answers will vary.

Write an exclamation.
Answers will vary.

e 33

ences that Run On

...hat includes more than one idea is called a **run-on sentence**. ...on sentence, separate the ideas into individual sentences.

My friend has a horse it is black and white.
...d: My friend has a horse. It is black and white.

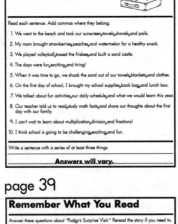

...entence. Circle the sentences that are written correctly. Rewrite the run-on ...two separate sentences.

...u seen her new haircut it is much shorter.
...ou seen her new haircut? It is much shorter.

...happy that it is my birthday I can't wait to open my presents.
...happy that it is my birthday. I can't wait to open my presents.

...time to go to the store yet we are leaving in ten minutes.
...time to go to the store yet. We are leaving in ten minutes.

...ang up your clothes and put your toys away.

...ere you yesterday did you go to the movie theater?
...were you yesterday? Did you go to the movie theater?

...ght a new car that is red and white.

...home yet I need to ask her a question.
...home yet? I need to ask her a question.

...g did it take you to make that was it difficult?
...ng did it take you to make that? Was it difficult?

...he is confusing it doesn't have directions.
...me is confusing. It doesn't have directions.

...g to the store do you need anything?
...ng to the store. Do you need anything?

page 34

Comma Consistency

Use a **comma** to separate words in a **series** (three or more things).

I packed my **shirt, pants, and socks**.

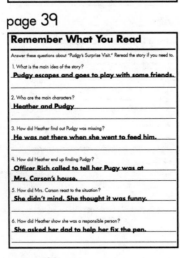

Read each sentence. Add commas where they belong.

1. We went to the beach and took our sunscreen, towels, shovels, and pails.
2. My mom brought strawberries, peaches, and watermelon for a healthy snack.
3. We played volleyball, tossed the frisbee, and built a sand castle.
4. The days were fun, exciting, and tiring!
5. When it was time to go, we shook the sand out of our towels, blankets, and clothes.
6. On the first day of school, I brought my school supplies, book bag, and lunch box.
7. We talked about fun activities, our daily schedule, and what we would learn this year.
8. Our teacher told us to read, study math facts, and share our thoughts about the first day with our family.
9. I can't wait to learn about multiplication, division, and fractions!
10. I think school is going to be challenging, exciting, and fun.

Write a sentence with a series of at least three things.
Answers will vary.

page 35

Make the Comma Connection

Use a **comma** between the name of a city and state and between the day and year.

I live in **Columbus, Ohio**.

We moved here on **July 28, 2001**.

Read each sentence. Add commas where they belong.

1. For vacation, my family went to Orlando, Florida.
2. The last time we were there was March 9, 2001.
3. We drove through Memphis, Tennessee.
4. Our hotel was just outside of Orlando in Kissimmee, Florida.
5. We arrived on December 23, 2002.
6. We spent a day at the beach in Orlando, Florida.
7. Then we spent a day at my aunt and uncle's house in Tampa, Florida.
8. Our family celebrated the New Year on January 1, 2003.
9. We checked out of the hotel on January 3, 2003.
10. On the way home, we visited our grandparents in Atlanta, Georgia.

What city and state do you live in?
Answers will vary.

What day where you born on?
Answers will vary.

page 36

Grammar is Great!

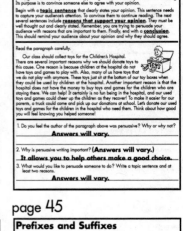

Underline all the nouns and circle all the verbs in each sentence.

1. Our class went on a field trip to the museum.
2. We played games and sang songs on the bus.
3. We arrived at the museum at 10:15.
4. The parent helper took us around the museum.
5. I enjoyed the field trip to the museum!

Read each sentence. Capitalize each proper noun and add commas where they belong.

6. lucy brown is one of my best friends. (**L**, **B**)
7. We like to play dolls, draw pictures, and put together puzzles.
8. I invited lucy and maddie over on saturday. (**L**, **M**, **S**)
9. we played, ate lunch, and helped Mrs. johnson with her garden. (**W**, **J**)
10. we planted petunias, impatiens, and roses. (**W**)

Write an adjective to describe each noun. **Answers will vary.**

______ apple   ______ pizza

______ park   ______ radio

______ pillow   ______ car

e 38

t in Order

...t the story "Pudgy's Surprise Visit."
...e sentences in the order that they happened
Reread the story if you need to.

Heather rushed to her mom to tell her that Pudgy was missing.

Heather went to Mrs. Carson's to get Pudgy.

Pudgy was a curious pig.

Heather went out to feed her pig and he was gone!

Heather asked her dad to help fix the pen so Pudgy would not get out.

Officer Rich called.

Pudgy was romping around in the grass with four tiny puppies.

...k Pudgy will make another special visit to his tiny puppy friends? ...y not?

No, because the cage is secured.

Answers will vary.

...your favorite part in the story? Describe it.

Answers will vary.

page 39

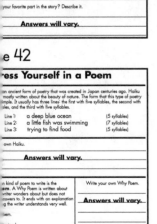

Remember What You Read

Answer these questions about "Pudgy's Surprise Visit." Reread the story if you need to.

1. What is the main idea of the story?
   Pudgy escapes and goes to play with some friends.
2. Who are the main characters?
   Heather and Pudgy
3. How did Heather find out Pudgy was missing?
   He was not there when she went to feed him.
4. How did Heather end up finding Pudgy?
   Officer Rich called to tell her Pugy was at Mrs. Carson's house.
5. How did Mrs. Carson react to the situation?
   She didn't mind. She thought it was funny.
6. How did Heather show she was a responsible person?
   She asked her dad to help her fix the pen.

page 40

What Do You Think?

Think about the story "Pudgy's Surprise Visit." Reread the story if you need to.

1. Draw a picture of the look on Heather's face when she found the empty pen.

   Drawings will vary.

2. Explain how you think she felt when she saw that Pudgy was not in his pen.
   Heather was probably surprised because this had never happened before.
   (Answers will vary.)
3. Describe what Heather might have done if Officer Rich hadn't called so quickly.
   Heather may have asked the neighbors if they saw Pudgy.
   (Answers will vary.)
4. What do you think Heather will do differently next time?
   Heather will probably double-check to make sure the pen is secured.
   (Answers will vary.)

page 41

Be Persuasive

Writing that states an opinion with supporting reasons is called **persuasive writing**. Its purpose is to convince someone else to agree with your opinion.

Begin with a **topic sentence** that clearly states your opinion. This sentence needs to capture your audience's attention. To convince them to continue reading. The next several sentences include **reasons that support your opinion**. They must be well thought out and clearly stated. Remember, you are trying to persuade your audience with reasons that are important to them. Finally, end with a **conclusion**. This should remind your audience about your opinion and why they should agree.

Read the paragraph carefully.

Our class should collect toys for the Children's Hospital. There are several important reasons why we should donate toys to this cause. One reason is because children at the hospital do not have toys and games to play with. Also, many of us have toys that we do not play with anymore. These toys just sit at the bottom of our toy boxes when they could be used by children at the hospital. Another important reason is that the hospital does not have the money to buy toys and games for the children who are staying there. We can help! It certainly is no fun being in the hospital, and our used toys and games could cheer up the children as they recover! To make it easier for our parents, a truck could come and pick up our donations at school. Let's donate our used toys and games for the children in the hospital who need them. Think about how good you will feel knowing you helped someone!

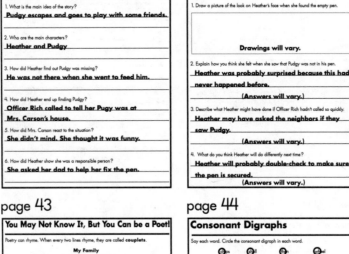

1. Do you feel the author of the paragraph above was persuasive? Why or why not?
   Answers will vary.
2. Why is persuasive writing important? **(Answers will vary.)**
   It allows you to help others make a good choice.
3. What would you like to persuade someone to do? Write a topic sentence and at least two reasons.
   Answers will vary.

e 42

ress Yourself in a Poem

...an ancient form of poetry that was created in Japan centuries ago. Haiku ...mostly written about the beauty of nature. The form that this type of poetry ...imple. It usually has three lines: the first with five syllables, the second with ...les, and the third with five syllables.

Line 1:	a deep blue ocean	(5 syllables)
Line 2:	a little fish was swimming	(7 syllables)
Line 3:	trying to find food	(5 syllables)

...own Haiku.

Answers will vary.

...n kind of poem to write is the ...em. A Why Poem is written about ...writer wonders about but does not ...nswers to. It ends with an explanation ...g the writer understands very well.

...oem.

...rstand
...people are homeless
...are people without food
...is violence in the world
...don't understand
...e can be unkind

...lerstand the most is that
...oves me and is proud of me
...ways do my best

Write your own Why Poem.

Answers will vary.

page 43

You May Not Know It, But You Can be a Poet!

Poetry can rhyme. When every two lines rhyme, they are called **couplets**.

My Family

Mom, your stories touch my day with laughter and a smile.
I appreciate your warmth and ever-loving style.

Billy, your gentleness adds a special touch to my day,
And your giving heart shows more to me than words could ever say.

Sara, your caring and sensitive side is special about you.
These qualities you hold will help in everything that you do.

Dad, you are a special friend with hugs for me each day.
You brighten up my life in such a fantastic way.

Write your own poem with couplets.

Answers will vary.

page 44

Consonant Digraphs

Say each word. Circle the consonant digraph in each word.

chips	shell	thin	wheel
fish	when	cherry	booth
with	chew	three	wh...

Underline the consonant digraph in each word. Then write a sentence using the word.

charity **Answers will vary.**

friendship **Answers will vary.**

theater **Answers will vary.**

whine **Answers will vary.**

wish **Answers will vary.**

Write the missing consonant digraph to complete each word. Then rewrite the word.

w **h** i l e — **while**

c **h** a l l e n g e — **challenge**

s **h** i n e — **shine**

s **h** a l l o w — **shallow**

t **h** r e a d — **thread**

page 45

Prefixes and Suffixes

Add a prefix or suffix to complete each word in the sentences.

prefixes	suffixes
un	er
re	est
pre	ful
	less

1. I went to the gas station to **re**fill my gas tank.
2. After I put lotion on my hands they were much soft**er**.
3. When you say thank you, you are showing people that you are respect**ful**.
4. The frown on his face told us that he was **un**happy.
5. We took a **pre**test to see how much we knew before we started the chapter.
6. When you are still and not moving, you are motion**less**.
7. One of the great**est** feelings is when someone shows they care about you.
8. She has good foot skills, which make her an excellent soccer play**er**.

Write a sentence using each word.

wonderful **Answers will vary.**

remake **Answers will vary.**

taller **Answers will vary.**

unsure **Answers will vary.**

Synonyms and Antonyms

Write a synonym and antonym for each underlined word. **(Answers may vary.)**

1. On _the_ last day of school, our _class_ was very _sad_.
Synonym: **unhappy**   Antonym: **happy**

2. We went to the park and had a _good_ time.
Synonym: **enjoyable**   Antonym: **bad**

3. My mother makes the _best_ chocolate cake.
Synonym: **greatest**   Antonym: **worst**

4. Sally turned down the volume on the television because she said it was too _loud_.
Synonym: **noisy**   Antonym: **quiet**

5. I was _glad_ to be done with that project.
Synonym: **happy**   Antonym: **sad**

6. The rainbow was _beautiful_ and colorful.
Synonym: **pretty**   Antonym: **ugly**

7. When he received the ribbon he looked very _excited_.
Synonym: **delighted**   Antonym: **disappointed**

8. I thanked my mom in a _quiet_ voice.
Synonym: **soft**   Antonym: **loud**

9. The bear was big and _scary_.
Synonym: **frightening**   Antonym: **friendly**

10. After the game, the players were _tired_.
Synonym: **exhausted**   Antonym: **energetic**

Main Idea and Details

Write the main idea and supporting details for each paragraph.

There are three main differences between butterflies and moths. First, butterflies are usually brightly colored and moths are usually dull in color. Second, butterflies are active during the day and moths are active at night. Third, butterflies form a chrysalis and moths form a cocoon.

Main idea **There are three main differences between butterflies and moths.**

Supporting details **Butterflies are usually brightly colored and moths are usually dull. Butterflies are active during the day and moths are active at night. Butterflies form chrysalis and moths form a cocoon.**

Toads and frogs have many differences. One difference is their skin. A toad's skin is warty and dry, but the skin of a frog is moist and smooth. Also, toads tend to walk, while frogs tend to jump. And toads and frogs have different-looking feet. Toads have almost no webbing on their feet, but frog feet are usually fully webbed. Another major difference is where they live. Toads typically live on land and away from water. Frogs, on the other hand, live in or near water.

Main idea **Toads and frogs have many differences**

Supporting details **A toad's skin is warty and dry, but the skin of a frog is moist and smooth. Toads have almost no webbing on their feet, but frog feet are fully webbed. Toads typically live on land and away from water. Frogs live in or near water.**

Descriptive Writing

Think about a special time that you shared with a family member, such as going fishing with Grandpa, going swimming with Mom, or planting flowers with an aunt. Write your special moment on the line.

My special moment is: **Answers will vary.**

Write some details about your special moment in the box.

Answers will vary.

Write a paragraph about your special moment using the supporting details.
Answers will vary.

Complete Sentences

Rewrite each group of words to make complete sentences.

1. the playground went to I
I went to the playground.

2. My aunt at the clothing store works
My aunt works at the clothing store.

3. monkey on the swing Do you see
Do you see the monkey on the swing?

4. movie Lynn and I on Saturday saw a
Lynn and I saw a movie on Saturday.

5. two big dogs next live door
Two big dogs live next door.

6. My favorite checkers game is
My favorite game is checkers.

7. driving a red bird saw my father while to work
My father saw a red bird while driving to work.

8. got wet socks my
My socks got wet.

9. decided to baseball play
We decided to play baseball.

10. home for a snack I came
I came home for a snack.

Run-on Sentences

Read each run-on sentence. Rewrite it as two separate sentences.

1. I like to play baseball I am on a team.
I like to play baseball. I am on a team.

2. We went to the field the game was cancelled because of rain.
We went to the field. The game was cancelled because of rain.

3. John was sad he wanted to try out his new baseball glove.
John was sad. He wanted to try out his new baseball glove.

4. We left the field Dad asked if we wanted to stop for ice cream.
We left the field. Dad asked if we wanted to stop for ice cream.

5. That surprised us we got to order a sundae or a cone.
That surprised us. We got to order a sundae or a cone.

6. I ordered a double scoop of chocolate Dad ordered vanilla.
I ordered a double scoop of chocolate. Dad ordered vanilla.

7. We had fun we ate at a picnic table.
We had fun. We ate at a picnic table.

8. It was time to go we thanked Dad!
It was time to go. We thanked Dad!

9. Dad said, "You're welcome" he enjoyed it, too.
Dad said, "You're welcome." He enjoyed it, too.

10. On the way home, we talked about baseball we talked about basketball, too.
On the way home, we talked about baseball. We talked about basketball, too.

Subjects and Predicates

Read each sentence. Circle the subject and underline the predicate.

1. (Our family) goes on a vacation every year.

2. (The best vacation) was when we went to Washington, D.C.

3. (We) saw so many historic sights.

4. (My favorite part) was the tour of the White House.

Add a subject to complete each sentence.

5. **Answers will vary.** went to the library.

6. **Answers will vary.** and I ride bicycles together.

7. **Answers will vary.** was late getting to work yesterday.

8. **Answers will vary.** sells three flavors of ice cream.

Add a predicate to complete each sentence.

9. The man **Answers will vary.**

10. Jerry and Jason **Answers will vary.**

11. Natalie **Answers will vary.**

12. The boat **Answers will vary.**

Three Parts of Speech

Read each sentence. Circle the nouns. Draw a box around the verbs.

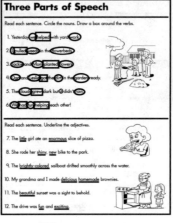

1. Yesterday we helped with yard work.

2. I pulled weeds in the flowerbeds.

3. Jackie and Mom planted flowers.

4. Ann and Leslie got the garden ready.

5. The clouds grew dark but it didn't rain.

6. We had fun helping each other!

Read each sentence. Underline the adjectives.

7. The _little_ girl ate an _enormous_ slice of pizza.

8. She rode her _shiny, new_ bike to the park.

9. The _brightly-colored_ sailboat drifted smoothly across the water.

10. My grandma and I made _delicious homemade_ brownies.

11. The _beautiful_ sunset was a sight to behold.

12. The drive was _fun_ and _exciting_.

Pronouns

Read each sentence. Circle all the pronouns.

1. (We) made pizza for dinner.

2. (It) tasted really good.

3. (We) added many ingredients to the pizza.

4. (I) wanted to put pepperoni on (it).

5. Rick wanted to put extra cheese on (it).

6. (He) also wanted sausage, but (we) didn't have any.

7. Dad said that (he) had a taste for mushrooms.

8. It was the best pizza (I) ever tasted.

9. Maybe (we) should open our own pizza shop.

10. (It) would probably be a lot of fun!

Write a pronoun that can take the place of the underlined nouns.

11. **We** _Rick and I_ had fun making pizza.

12. **it** Dad helped us make _the pizza_.

13. **He** _Dad_ had lots of fun, too.

14. **They** _My mom and sister_ asked for a slice.

15. **She** _My sister_ didn't like the mushrooms.

Capitals and Punctuation

Read the sentences. Rewrite them using capital letters and punctuation.

1. yesterday we went to the swimming pool
Yesterday we went to the swimming pool.

2. jeff and i got really tired from swimming a lot
Jeff and I got really tired from swimming a lot.

3. do you know what i liked best about the day
Do you know what I liked best about the day?

4. i loved the water slide
I loved the water slide!

5. sometimes the line for the slide was long
Sometimes the line for the slide was long.

6. ashly can dive very well
Ashley can dive very well.

7. did you see ashly dive
Did you see Ashley dive?

8. mom brought healthy snacks for us to eat
Mom brought healthy snacks for us to eat.

9. the snacks helped give us energy
The snacks helped give us energy.

10. we all had so much fun
We all had so much fun!

Commas

Read each sentence. Add commas where they belong.

1. For my birthday, I am having a party with my family, friends, and neighbors.

2. I invited Ian, Adam, and Eric.

3. Robbie, Joseph, and Noah are coming, too.

4. We are going to play volleyball, have a water balloon toss, and go swimming.

5. You need to take your time, throw carefully, and concentrate during the balloon toss.

6. For lunch we are having hamburgers, cheeseburgers, and hotdogs.

7. I love cheeseburgers with ketchup, mustard, and pickles.

8. Dad likes his with lettuce, onions, and tomatoes, too.

9. We also are having potato salad, baked beans, and pasta salad.

10. Dessert is a sundae with strawberry, chocolate, and vanilla ice cream!

11. I am looking forward to opening my gifts and playing with my friends.

12. Aunt Betty, Aunt Rose, and Uncle Len each brought a present for me.

13. One present is from Mom, Dad, and Bobby.

14. I am really hoping to get a new bike, a helmet, and a raft for the pool.

15. Parties are great because family, friends, and neighbors get to visit with each other!

Story Details and Sequence

Think about the story "Sugar and Spice." Number the sentences in the order that they happened in the story. Reread the story if you need to.

6 Michelle got Sugar as an early birthday present.

1 Michelle and Ryan stopped by the pet shop once a week.

4 Michelle went to Ryan's birthday party.

2 Michelle and Ryan got busy at school and home and could not stop by the pet shop.

5 Ryan opened his last present. It was Spice!

3 Michelle and her mom passed by the pet shop and saw that Spice was not there.

Do you think Sugar and Spice will continue to be best friends? Why or why not?
Yes, because their owners are friends they will get to play together
(Answers will vary.)

What was your favorite part in the story? Describe it.
(Answers will vary.)

What Do You Remember?

Answer these questions about "Sugar and Spice." Reread the story if you ne

1. What is the main idea of the story?
Sugar and Spice are best friend who are separated but in the end are back together.

2. Who are the main characters?
Sugar, Spice, Michelle, and Ryan

3. How did Michelle and Ryan feel about Sugar and Spice?
They really like to see them. They have fun with them.
(Answers will vary.)

4. Why did Michelle and Ryan stop going to the pet shop after school?
They didn't have time.

5. How did Michelle react when she and her mom did not see Spice at the
She was very sad and felt like crying.

6. How do you think Michelle and Ryan feel about their new kittens?
They were excited because they can be together again
(Answers will vary.)

Predict the Outcome

Think about the story "Sugar and Spice." Reread the story if you need to.

1. Draw a picture of the look on Ryan's and Michelle's faces when they opened their presents and saw Sugar and Spice.

Drawings will vary.

2. Explain how you think they felt when they saw Sugar and Spice together again.
Answers will vary.

3. Describe how you think Ryan's feelings changed after Michelle opened her early birthday present.
Answers will vary.

4. Who do you think is happier, Ryan and Michelle or Sugar and Spice? Why?
Answers will vary.

Persuasive Writing

1. List some ideas of things that you would like to persuade someone to do.
Answers will vary.
• **make his/her bed**   • **donate money**
• **clean his/her room**   • **donate time**
• **wash the dishes**   • **wash the car**
• **donate food**   • **clean the garage**

2. Choose one idea and write a persuasive letter.

Dear **Answers will vary.**

I think you should _____

There are several reasons why this is a good idea. One reason is _____

Another reason is _____

Finally, _____

Just think about how good you will feel _____

Sincerely,

Answers